Fundamental

TENNIS

Coach Marc Miller and the following athletes were photographed for this book:
Ryan Burnet,
Charissa Coleman,
Christina Coleman,
Ryan Ford,
Neil Kolatkar,
Molly Purdy,
Heidi Rovick,
Charlie Schultz,
Mary Beth Schultz,
Philip Woo.

Fundamental
TENNIS

Marc Miller

Photographs by Andy King

Lerner Publications Company ● Minneapolis

To all the great teachers who have shaped my life: Don George, Ohama Shihan, Miura Shihan, Steve Wilkinson, Mom and Dad, Anne and Hunter.

Library of Congress Cataloging-in-Publication Data

Miller, Marc.
    Fundamental tennis/Marc Miller ; photographs by Andy King.
      p. cm. — (Fundamental sports)
    Includes bibliographical references (p.) and index.
    ISBN 0–8225–3450–9
    1. Tennis—Juvenile literature. [1. Tennis.] I. King, Andy, ill. II. Title. III. Series.
GV996.5.M55 1994
796.342—dc20
                              93–48385
                              CIP
                              AC
                              Rev.

Manufactured in the United States of America

1 2 3 4 5 6 - I/HP - 99 98 97 96 95

The Fundamental Sports series was conceptualized by editor Julie Jensen, designed by graphic artist Michael Tacheny, and composed on a Macintosh computer by Robert Mauzy.

Photo Acknowledgments
Photographs are reproduced with the permission of: p. 7, The Bettman Archive; p. 8, (top) The International Tennis Hall of Fame and Tennis Museum at the Newport Casino, Newport, R.I.; (bottom) The Bettman Archive; p. 9, (top) Sportschrome East/ West, Rob Tringali, Jr.; (bottom) Sportschrome East/West, Gilbert lundt; p. 55, UPI/Bettman.

Contents

Chapter 1

How This Game Got Started

Imagine yourself standing on a tennis court. Across the net from you is your opponent—who weighs 250 pounds and stands 6 feet, 3 inches tall. Frightening images flash through your mind.

In basketball or football you would be in trouble, but this is tennis. Tennis is a sport of action and explosive, changing movement. Size and weight aren't important when playing tennis. A skilled tennis player must be agile and fast, with quick hands and feet.

A tennis player also must have a strong and sharp mind. To have a solid game, a tennis player must focus on what is to be done next, anticipate an opponent's shots, and stay cool and calm under pressure.

THE ART AND SKILL

OF

LAWN TENNIS.

By B. HARDWICK.

REPRINTED FROM THE CENTURY MAGAZINE.

JOHN WANAMAKER,
GRAND DEPOT,
PHILADELPHIA, Pa.

An early tennis brochure

Major Walter Clopton Wingfield

"Tennis—The Sport of a Lifetime" is the motto of the United States Tennis Association (USTA). Youngsters can begin playing tennis when they are 2 or 3 years old, and adults have been known to play into their nineties. Because of this, tennis is a fantastic sport to learn and master.

As with many other sports, the exact origins of tennis are a bit sketchy. The first matches probably were played on stone courts with rocklike balls. When rubber balls were invented in 1850, the game of tennis changed forever. Tennis, as it is played today, was invented in England in 1873 by Major Walter Clopton Wingfield. He named the game sphairistike—which is Greek for "playing ball"—but called it "sticky" for short. One year later, Mary Ewing Outerbridge set up the first court in the United States, in New York City.

In 1881 the United States Lawn Tennis Association was formed by 33 tennis clubs. The name of the organization was later changed to the United States Tennis Association (USTA). The USTA has more than half a million members, and an estimated 22 million Americans play tennis.

The USTA sponsors and trains the United States' Olympic athletes and hosts the U.S. Open Tennis Championships each year. In addition, the USTA promotes programs for youth and adults to help in their development as players. Great American players such as Jimmy Connors, John McEnroe, Chris Evert, Jennifer Capriati, and Andre Agassi developed through the USTA program.

Chris Evert

Chris Evert was one of the greatest women tennis players in the history of the sport. Her father, James Evert, was a tennis professional and began giving her lessons when she was 6 years old. They would go down to the local park and he would toss balls to her. In the beginning, Chris missed nearly every ball, but soon she was showing signs of great talent.

Chris played in her first tournament when she was 8 years old. By the time she was 12, she was ranked second in the girls' 12-and-under age group in the United States. Two years later, she was the top-ranked player in the 14-and-under age group.

Chris entered her first professional tournament as a 15-year-old. She played as an amateur because in 1970 players could not turn pro until they were 18 years old. In that tournament, Chris upset the French champion, Francoise Durr, and then beat Margaret Court. This was considered a huge upset because Court had just won the Grand Slam—winning the French Open, Wimbledon, the U.S. Open, and the Australian Open in the same year.

Few athletes have ever dominated a sport like Chris did before she retired, and she always maintained the highest levels of sportsmanship. She was kind and considerate on and off the court. Chris will be remembered as a great tennis player, but more importantly, she will serve as a model of sportsmanship and integrity.

Andre Agassi at the French Open

Chapter 2

BASICS

The basic idea of tennis is simple: hit the ball over the net and inside the **court,** and do this one more time than your opponent does. The court is 78 feet long and 27 feet wide for playing **singles**. Singles is tennis that is played by two players, one against one. Across the middle of the court is a net that is 3 feet high in the middle and 3½ feet high at the net posts. When four players are playing two-on-two, or **doubles,** they use the **doubles alleys,** which extend 4½ feet on each side of the court.

Lines on the court show players where certain shots need to be hit. The most important lines are the **singles sidelines,** the **doubles sidelines,** the **service line,** and the **baseline.**

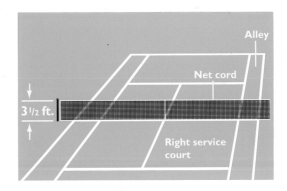

Balls

Tennis balls are about 2½ inches in diameter, and weigh about 2 ounces. They are hollow, and their rubber frame is covered with a fabric made of nylon and wool.

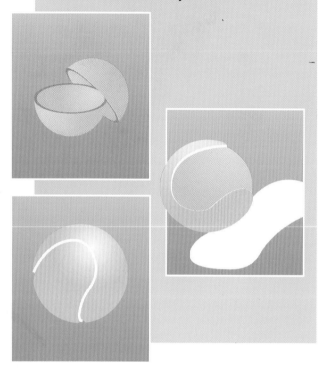

Styles of Play

*The way that players play tennis depends on the surface on which they are playing. Surfaces like clay are rough, which slows the ball down and gives it a higher bounce. These courts are called **slow courts.** To win consistently on slow courts, a player must be steady and in good physical shape. Points on slow surfaces last a long time and involve many hits.*

*Surfaces like grass are slick, so the ball bounces low and fast, which leads to the name **fast courts.** On fast courts, players need to be strong enough to hit the ball hard and deep. Fast-court points are shorter in length, so players must be able to finish points quickly by hitting hard and attacking.*

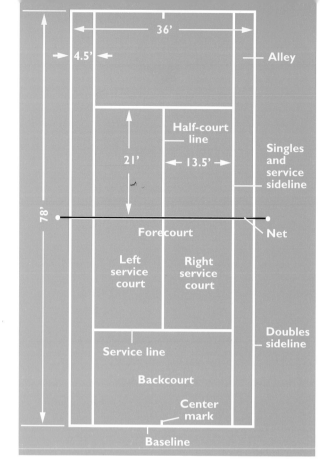

The Court

When Major Wingfield introduced tennis to the world, most matches were played on grass courts and the game was first called "lawn tennis." But just like your backyard, grass courts needed to be mowed and watered. Because grass courts were expensive to maintain, other court surfaces were developed.

Today, tennis is played—indoors and outdoors—on many surfaces, including concrete, asphalt, clay (dirt), grass, and even on indoor carpet. The type of surface used depends on the weather and the materials available where the courts are to be built. For example, in India there is very little clay to build clay courts. Therefore some courts are made of cow poop that is rolled and made flat and hard. This makes a great tennis court surface but gets a little smelly when it rains!

Strings

Most rackets do not come with strings when purchased. Strings are made from many materials. The most common string today is synthetic gut string made from nylon. Rackets can be purchased for as little as $30 or as much as $300. Having a racket strung usually costs between $15 and $30.

If possible, have your racket strung by someone certified by the United States Professional Racquet Stringers Association. These professionals will know the best type of string and string tension for you and your racket. When selecting a new racket, ask a certified professional for help. They will be able to match the correct racket to your body type and size.

The Racket

Before ever going to the court, a player must choose a **racket**. Rackets come in many shapes and sizes, but most are about 27 inches long. Most rackets are built using several types of materials, such as fiberglass and graphite, layered together. Using many layers not only gives the racket strength and power, but also keeps it lightweight so the player can swing it rapidly. Racket handles come in different sizes, so that all players are able to find a racket they can hold comfortably. The hitting surface of a racket is a tightly strung net of nylon or other synthetic strings.

The Clothes

When going out to practice tennis, a player should wear loose-fitting clothes—like shorts, a T-shirt, and tennis shoes—that will allow quick, explosive movement. Wearing light-colored clothing, which reflects the sun's rays, will help keep you cool on hot days.

Shoes are the most important part of a tennis player's clothing. Shoes should fit well to prevent blisters and should be supportive so that a player's ankles and knees are not injured. Running shoes are not good for playing tennis because they are not built for the quick side-to-side movements tennis players must make. Tennis shoes should have good traction so that players do not slip and fall during play.

Socks

Because tennis players have to change direction so often, socks also are important. Many players wear two pairs of socks to prevent blisters. In general, thick socks made of cotton are best for tennis.

Open racket face

Closed racket face

Flat racket face

Racket Faces

If the strings of the racket face up, the racket face is called open. When the strings face down, the racket face is closed. When the strings face straight ahead, the racket face is called flat.

*Most tennis strokes should be hit with a flat racket face. The best way to get a flat racket face is to hold the racket correctly. The way a player holds his or her racket is called a **grip**.*

The Strokes

Once you have the necessary equipment, you can learn the basic techniques, or **strokes,** of tennis. Remember, your goal in tennis is to hit the ball over the net and into your opponent's side of the court so that he or she can't hit it back to you. To do this, you need to be able to do the following moves. Four strokes form the foundation of a tennis game: the **serve,** the **ground strokes (forehand** and **backhand**), and the **volley**.

The serve is the only stroke that you begin by yourself. All other strokes are hit after your opponent hits, which means that you are usually running to make these strokes. When you're in motion, it is often difficult to hit the ball exactly where you want it.

Ground strokes—shots that are hit after the ball bounces on your side of the court—are hit from both the forehand and backhand sides. Right-handed players hit a forehand on their right side and reach across their bodies to hit a backhand. Left-handed players hit a forehand on their left side and reach across their bodies to hit a backhand on the right side.

Ground strokes can be hit from anywhere on the court but are usually hit from near the baseline. Groundstrokes are usually hit **crosscourt** (from one corner of the court diagonally across to another corner) because the court is longer that way, and the net is lower in the middle.

The other stroke to learn is the volley. Volleys are hit before the ball bounces on your side of the court, which means that volleys generally are hit near the net. Volleys tend to be more of a "punching" motion rather than a full swing or stroke.

Grips and the Grip Line

The line drawn on Ryan's hand from the base of his index finger to the pad of his hand shows the grip line. This is the line used to find the correct grip for each stroke. All racket handles have eight sides. To identify these edges, imagine that the end of a racket is a clock. The top edge of the racket is at the 12:00, and the next edge to the right is between the 1:00 and the 2:00. The next two edges are at the 3:00 and between the 4:00 and 5:00. The fifth edge is at the 6:00. To find the correct grips for the strokes, match the grip line on your hand to the correct side of the racket (clock).

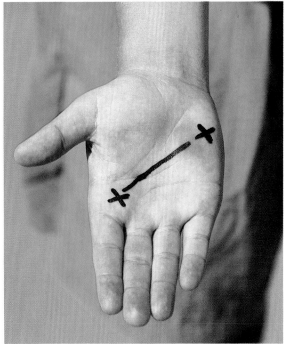

If Ryan puts his grip line at 12:00, he has an Eastern Backhand grip. When the grip line is between the 1:00 and the 2:00, the grip is a Continental grip. At the 3:00, the grip is an Eastern Forehand grip, and when the grip line is between the 4:00 and 5:00 the grip is called Semi-Western. A grip that is all the way below the handle at the 6:00 is called a Western grip.

The Serve

Most players use a Continental grip when they serve, although an Eastern Forehand grip works fine too. The service motion is a throwing motion, which means if you can throw a ball, you should be able to serve. There are two basic parts to the serve—the toss and the swing.

When you begin learning the serve, picture the perfect serve before you begin. Watch a professional match on TV to find a model for your perfect serve. Remember, the serve is one long, fluid motion, not a bunch of little pieces. Try to fix a good, long motion in your mind before beginning the serve.

The Stance

This is the **stance,** or beginning position, for the serve. Ryan is not facing his target on the other side of the court in this position, but is sideways to the target with his left shoulder pointing toward the net. Ryan is right-handed; if he were left-handed, his right shoulder would point toward the net. Ryan's arms are loose and relaxed and hanging down by his hips.

The Toss

The toss is the most important part of the serve. If you develop a consistent toss and have a strong throwing motion, then you will develop a strong serve. The toss should be just high enough so that it goes to the maximum height that you are able to reach with your racket.

Release the ball only when your tossing arm is stretched as high as it can go. Then the ball should go only about one foot out of your hand before it is hit. Think of it this way: If someone asked you to toss 100 balls into a bucket that was only a foot away from you, how many balls would you make in the bucket? Probably 100! What if you had to toss the balls in a bucket that was five feet away? If you release the ball from waist high when serving, you have to toss the ball four to five feet. This makes the toss inconsistent.

Look again at Ryan's serve. He has released the ball from the highest point with his arm stretched toward the sky. In addition to being the right height, the ball also should be a little bit in front and a little bit to the right (for a right-handed player) of the front foot. If Ryan lets the ball get behind his head, he is going to have problems. Keep the toss out in front!

The V Position

At the same time that the toss is released, the racket arm also must be getting into position. Remember, the ball is only going to go into the air one foot, so the racket must be in position to hit right after the toss is released. To do this, both arms must come up together, forming the **V position**.

Ryan's left hand has released the toss and his racket hand is up and ready to swing at the ball. This is the classic position for the serve. In fact, it is so classic that most tennis trophies have a figure in this position at the top of the trophy!

Over the Net

The back-scratch position allows the server to hit up into the ball on the serve. You would need to be 13½ feet tall and have an oversized racket in order to be able to hit down on the ball and still get it over the net and into the service box. Because no one is 13½ feet tall, we must hit up on the ball to get it over the net. Gravity and a little bit of spin allow for the ball to be hit up and still land in the service box for a good serve.

The Rhythm of the Serve

Once a player establishes a feel for the serve, the key to pulling it together is rhythm. Let's call the ball toss and the V position #1, the back-scratch position #2, and the point of contact #3. If we were counting out these numbers during a good, fluid serve we would say, "..1.......2.3." Keep the first part of the motion slow and easy (..1.....) because that will make the ball toss accurate and consistent. But once the ball is released, go as fast as possible (..2.3.).

The back-scratch position and the point of contact happen quickly. The faster the motion, the harder the ball will be hit. Keep in mind that it is not the size of your muscles that makes the ball go fast. It is the speed of the racket that gives the ball zip.

The Back-Scratch Position

The **back-scratch position** is called that because the racket moves from the V position down the back, as if the server were using the racket as a back-scratcher. This happens as the server rotates forward toward the target. Be sure you let the racket "fall" down your back as your body turns forward. If you are doing a throwing motion, the racket will naturally go down your back. If you try to force the racket down your back, your service motion will become choppy and weak. Let the racket naturally fall down your back.

The Point of Contact

The **point of contact** is the place where the ball and the racket actually meet. This point should be as high as you can reach with your racket and out in front of the baseline a little bit. Ryan is reaching for the ball at the point of contact. See how his eyes are still focusing on the ball. One of the most common mistakes that players make is looking to see where the ball is going to go before hitting it. This causes players to hit the ball on the frame of the racket, called a **mis-hit**, instead of in the center of the racket on the strings.

The Finish

After the ball is hit, the **finish** for the serve should be long and smooth. The racket hand should finish so your thumb ends up on your left pocket (right pocket for a lefty). Ryan's hand has finished across his body near his left pocket. Most servers will finish inside the baseline about two or three feet. This is because when reaching this high for the ball, your body weight and momentum will carry you forward into the court. If you have done your serve correctly and have placed the ball toss in front of your body, then your momentum should carry you in the direction of your serve. If your momentum carries you sideways, your ball toss was off to the side one way or the other.

The Recovery

Even though your serve is completed, you are not finished. After hitting the serve, you need to **recover** your court position. If you stand two or three feet inside the baseline after your serve, you will not be in position for your opponent's return. Immediately after hitting the serve, shuffle back to your ready position about one foot behind the baseline and near the middle of the court. Then you will be ready to hit your next shot.

Ground strokes–Forehand and Backhand

Whether hitting a forehand or a back-hand, your biggest obstacle is the net. Some players look at the net and say, "But the net is only three feet high! I can hit the ball over that." Tennis players who think like that usually do not do very well when they go out to play.

At all levels of play, from beginning to world class, most of the mistakes made are balls hit into the net. Hit the ball three or four feet above the net every time to avoid this costly mistake.

Low-to-High

Forehands and backhands are hit with a low-to-high motion. At the start of the swing, the racket is below the ball (low). By the end of the swing, the racket finishes above the ball (high). This motion produces a lifting action that sends the ball over the net.

At the same time, the racket face must be flat. If the racket becomes open and hits the bottom of the ball, the ball will fly beyond the baseline and land outside the lines. With the racket flat, the ball is lifted over the net but lands inside the baseline.

The Ready Position

While waiting to hit any of these shots, get your body in the **ready position**. Your knees should be comfortably bent and your weight should be slightly on the balls of your feet. Your grip should be loose and relaxed, and your racket should be about waist high. Neil is in a great ready position, waiting for his next shot.

The Forehand
The Grip

The grip used for the forehand is some-times called the "shake hands" grip because it resembles shaking hands with the racket. The official name is the Eastern Forehand grip. Notice how the grip line is on the racket handle at the 3:00 position. If you need to review the grip line or the racket edges, turn to page 15.

The Preparation

As you prepare to hit a forehand shot, think of hitting the stroke with your whole body. Think of your body turning sideways as your racket goes back. Neil has turned sideways to the net in prep-aration for the stroke. His racket is point-ing to the back fence and his eyes are focused on the ball. Neil's legs are slight-ly bent and his body is well balanced.

The Point of Contact

As the stroke begins, Neil's racket head drops below the ball so that he'll be able to stroke the ball with a low-to-high motion. The racket moves forward toward the ball because Neil's hips and shoulders have rotated forward toward the net. Remember, use your whole body to hit the stroke. If Neil hit this ball with only his arm, his stroke would be wimpy. He turns his hips and shoulders into the ball so that his stroke will be strong.

The ball and racket meet at a position that is even with his front foot. At this point the racket face is flat and Neil's eyes are focused on the ball. As the racket moves forward to the ball, Neil's weight also shifts slightly to his front foot.

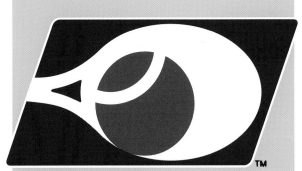

UNITED STATES TENNIS ASSOCIATION NATIONAL JUNIOR TENNIS LEAGUE

A League of Your Own

One of the best ways to start playing tennis is to join the USTA's National Junior Tennis League (NJTL). The League was founded in 1968 by Arthur Ashe. The primary goal of the NJTL is to introduce young athletes to tennis through teamwork, cooperation, and competition.

NJTL teachers and instructors work hard to see that all boys and girls in the program have fun. Young athletes also learn and improve skills, make new friends, stay physically fit, and enjoy the excitement of tennis.

There are more than 500 NJTL chapters across the United States, so finding one near you should be easy. To locate your nearest NJTL program, contact the USTA.

The Finish

As Neil strokes the ball, he extends his racket out toward the target. Instead of thinking about hitting one ball, Neil should picture hitting 10 balls in a line to his target. By doing this, Neil will develop accuracy and control with his forehand. After hitting through his 10 imaginary balls, Neil's racket will go up and over his left shoulder. Neil should be able to look directly over his hitting elbow and see his target on the other side of the net. A good low-to-high motion will assure that Neil hits the ball over the net. Neil is in a balanced position during this finish.

The Recovery

Because Neil finishes balanced and controlled, he can quickly recover his position and get ready for the next shot. Neil should recover by using shuffling steps, moving his feet side to side. In general, don't cross your feet when you recover your court position, because it is difficult to change directions with your feet crossed. If you shuffle, you can change directions and run for the next shot with ease. Because Neil is not going to the net now, he should get back into a position about one foot behind the baseline.

Backhands

There are two ways of hitting backhands—with both hands or with one hand, as for a forehand. Many players use both hands for more power and better control. Others choose to use one hand for quicker shots and a longer reach.

Two-Handed Backhand
The Grip

The grip for the two-handed backhand is actually two forehand grips, one with each hand. Heidi is using this grip.

The Preparation

As with the forehand, a player prepares for this shot by turning his or her body and pulling back the racket. The racket should point to the back fence and the shoulders should be sideways to the net. Notice Heidi's racket in this position. She will be able to easily swing the racket along a low-to-high path. Heidi's eyes are focused on the ball and her legs and body are low. Now she can explode into the ball when the swing begins.

The point of contact

The Point of Contact

After this great preparation, Heidi rotates her hips and shoulders toward the net. This pulls her racket forward so that she hits the ball when it is even with her front foot. Heidi's racket face is flat, and her eyes are focused on the ball.

The Finish

Heidi's legs are straightening as she finishes. This shows how she uses her entire body and not just her arms to hit the ball. Her racket finishes high and above her right shoulder. She can look over her left elbow and see her target on the opponent's court. She is also balanced in this position so that her recovery will be quick and explosive.

The Recovery

Heidi does not stand and admire her backhand. If she did, her opponent could hit the ball to the other side, and Heidi would not be able to get it. Instead, Heidi immediately shuffles back near the middle of the court. She stays on her toes and positions herself about one foot behind the baseline.

The finish

One-Handed Backhand
The Grip

Most players hitting a one-handed backhand use an Eastern Backhand grip. To form this grip, the player should place the grip line on the 12:00 edge of the racket handle. Some players rotate this grip over a little and use a Continental grip instead. Look at page 15 and compare the Eastern Backhand and Continental grips.

The Preparation

As his opponent hits the ball, Charlie rotates his shoulders back. Because he was waiting with a forehand grip, he uses his left hand to help him change his grip to a backhand grip. His shoulders rotate until they are sideways to the net. Charlie's eyes are focused on the ball in front of him.

The Point of Contact

To begin the stroke, Charlie will step toward the ball and pull the racket forward with his shoulders. Charlie's arms begin to spread so that the racket goes forward to meet the ball. The point of contact on a one-handed backhand is 1 to 1½ feet in front of the front foot. You can see that Charlie's left hand is moving toward the back fence away from the racket hand. This will allow Charlie to keep his racket moving in line with the target.

The Finish

Charlie's arms have spread apart and his body is still sideways to the net at the finish. His racket finishes high above his head and his weight is balanced over his feet. From this position he shuffles back toward the middle of the court, ready for the next shot.

Volley
Court Position

A volley is hit before the ball bounces. It is an attacking stroke used to finish the point and can be hit from the forehand or backhand sides. The volley generally is hit from halfway between the net and the service line.

The Grip

The volley grip is the same as that used for the ground strokes. More advanced players often use a Continental grip, which allows the player to use the same grip for both forehands and backhands. Volleying tends to be quick because the play is so close to the net.

The Preparation

When volleying, keep your racket in front of your body with your racket head up. Play at the net is so quick there is no time to recover if your racket is behind you even a little bit. Your first move when volleying is to point the racket face at the ball.

The Point of Contact

The point of contact for the volley is in front of and away from your body. Because the volley doesn't require a swing, the power comes from stepping into the ball with the racket in front. Neil is stepping into the ball as he gets ready to hit the forehand volley. On many volleys, you must take several steps just to get to the ball. Mary is moving several steps to hit this backhand volley. Both Neil and Mary have their eyes glued to the ball as they hit.

The Finish

There is no finish on the volley. For accurate and solid volleys, the racket face should point to the target after the ball leaves the racket. Most volley points are won by volleying the ball to a spot that an opponent cannot reach. Hitting the volley hard is usually not necessary, especially if the volley is hit accurately. After hitting the volley, recover your court position so that you can hit the next ball.

Keep in mind when hitting any of these shots that accuracy and consistency are crucial. Nobody has ever won a tennis match! Does that surprise you? What this means is that most points in a match are scored on errors by the players. Become a player who makes few errors, and you are likely to take home many tennis trophies.

Chapter 3

SINGLES

Charlie stands behind the baseline, gazing across the net at his opponent. He calls out the score, "40-30," knowing that with one more point he'll win the match. He tosses the ball gently into the air and then, with blazing speed, he throws the head of his racket up to the ball. The serve is well hit and the ball skids off of the service line to Phil's left side. Phil lunges to the side with his eyes keenly on the ball, and he guides a solid forehand down the line deep into Charlie's court.

Charlie runs to the ball with his racket prepared for a backhand. As he nears the ball, his body begins to unwind and he lifts the ball deep into Phil's court. Phil, not expecting such a deep crosscourt return, finds himself running full speed to catch up to the ball, but he is too late. Charlie wins! Both players meet at the net, shake hands, and congratulate each other on a fantastic match.

This is the game of singles—two players matching their skills against each other. In addition to playing, the players have to keep track of the score themselves and call all of their own lines.

Playing by the Rules

Tennis is a sport of honesty and integrity. In most tennis matches, the players must act as umpires and referees and decide whether the ball lands inside or outside of the lines on their side of the court. All balls that are not clearly outside the line must be called "in."

Even the fans watching tennis matches behave differently than other sports fans. Spectators are quiet while tennis players play. All cheering, clapping, and encouraging is done between points

Any player who wants to play competitively should have a USTA Code of Conduct card. This card explains some of the rules of tennis and the behavior that is expected of all players. These cards are available through the USTA. See page 62 for the address of the USTA office.

Both players have to watch the ball carefully. A ball is in when it lands inside or touches the singles line. A ball is out when it lands clearly outside of the singles lines. Players do not call "in" when balls are in, but they do call "out" when the balls are out. If a player is even a little doubtful about whether a ball is in or out, the ball should be called in. Only when the ball is clearly outside the line should it be called out.

There are a few other rules that must be followed when playing tennis. The ball is allowed to bounce only once on your side of the court. When the ball bounces twice on your side, you should stop playing and give the point to your opponent. If you touch the net at any time during the point, you lose the point. You also cannot reach over the net to hit the ball.

Sometimes a ball will hit the top of the net and still go over. On a serve, this is called a **let** and the server gets to serve again for a replay. If it happens during the point, then the opponent must run forward and return the ball to the other side. Let's say that during the point Charlie and Phil just played, a ball from the next court rolls onto Charlie and Phil's court. If Charlie and Phil continue to play, there is a chance that one of them could step on the ball and injure himself. Therefore, whoever sees the ball rolling onto the court should stop the point by yelling "Let." This means that the point stops and is replayed. This kind of let can be called by either player when anything rolls or blows onto the court during play. This helps to keep players from getting hurt.

Scoring

Before you and your opponent can start a game, you must decide who will serve first and on which side of the court you will play. Players switch sides after each game.

One way to make these decisions is with a racket toss. One player spins a racket upright on the frame of the racket head. The other player says "Heads" —the racket manufacturer's logo up— or "Tails"—the logo down. If the racket lands the way the player guessed, that player can choose to serve or to pick the side he or she wants to play on first. If the racket lands the other way, the player who spun the racket gets to choose.

Scoring in tennis has not changed much since the creation of the game. A player scores a point when the opponent lets the ball bounce twice on his or her side, when the opponent hits the ball into the net or outside the court, or when the opponent touches the ball.

A game begins with both players having zero points. In tennis, zero is called **love**. The points in a game of tennis are: love, 15, 30, 40, and game. The server calls out the score before each serve, giving his or her score first.

Those terms don't make a lot of sense, but knowing that you're keeping score the way players did many years ago makes it kind of fun.

How Long Does a Tennis Match Last?

One of the most difficult things about playing tennis is that a player never knows quite how long he or she will be playing. In basketball or football, the length of the game is determined by a clock. In tennis, players play until the match is finished. The average tennis match lasts between 1-2 hours, but some matches are finished in 25-30 minutes. Other matches can last for hours and hours.

Two women, Vicky Nelson and Jean Hepner, played a match that lasted 6 hours and 22 minutes in a tournament in Richmond, Virginia, in October 1985. These players had one point that lasted for 643 hits. Each player hit the ball 322 times before the point ended! Vicky Nelson won the match in two sets, 6-4, 7-6. The match-ending tie-breaker (played to seven points with one player winning by two points) lasted 1 hour and 47 minutes and was finished at 13-11. That's a lot of tennis!

A player wins a **game** by winning at least four points and having at least two more points than his or her opponent. If Charlie is serving and wins the first point, the score is 15-love. The server always calls his or her score first. If Charlie also wins the second point, the score is 30-love. If he wins the third point, the score becomes 40-love. If he wins the last point, he wins the game.

If the players get to 40-40, the score is called **deuce**. To win a deuce game, a player must win two points in a row.

Charlie is serving with the score 40-40. Charlie calls "Deuce" and serves the ball wide to Phil's forehand. Phil leaps and hits the ball, but it sails beyond the baseline. Now the score is **ad-in,** the server has the advantage.

On the next point, Phil rips a backhand crosscourt and Charlie hits the ball into the net. Phil wins the point and the score is back to deuce. At deuce, Charlie hits both of his serves out, so Phil wins the point. Then the score is **ad-out,** because the server's opponent (Phil) has the advantage.

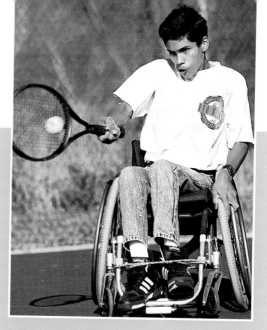

Charlie calls "Ad-out" and serves. Phil hits a short ball that Charlie lets bounce twice. Phil wins the point and, because he has won two consecutive points, he wins the game.

The first person to win six games, and at least two games more than his or her opponent, wins a **set**. If players tie the score at 6-6 in any set, then a **tie-breaker** is played. In a tie-breaker, players play 12 points. The first player to win seven points, and at least two more than his or her opponent, wins.

Let's say that Phil is leading the set 6-5. Even though Phil has won six games, the set would not be over because he is not leading by two games. If Phil won the next game, the score would be 7-5 and Phil would win the set.

Most **matches** are best-of-three sets—the first player to win two sets wins the match.

Wheelchair Tennis

Tennis is played by many different people from different backgrounds and different parts of the world. Tennis can be played by athletes of different physical abilities too. In fact, many people in wheelchairs play exceptionally good tennis.

The rules for wheelchair tennis are slightly different. The wheelchair player can let the ball bounce twice. The first bounce must be inside the court boundaries and the second bounce can be anywhere. Players are allowed to fix their chairs if they break during play. When serving, a wheelchair player must keep the rear wheels of the chair behind the baseline until the ball is hit.

Wheelchair athletes hit the same shots—forehands, backhands, volleys, and serves—as able-bodied players do. The obvious difference in wheelchair tennis is in moving to the ball. Wheelchair players move to where they can hit the ball on the second bounce. The ball is moving slower then, and is usually in a more comfortable contact zone for their strokes. Wheelchair players are not allowed to come out of their seats to hit any shots. This means that positioning is extremely important.

If you are in a wheelchair or know of someone who is, tennis is just the sport for you. The National Foundation of Wheelchair Tennis will be able to help you get involved with tennis. The foundation has books and videotapes that illustrate proper wheelchair tennis techniques. The foundation also can give you the names and phone numbers of local wheelchair tennis programs. Contact the USTA and get those wheels rolling!

The Server

The server begins every point in a tennis match. Molly is standing behind the baseline, just to the right of the middle line, to begin the point. She must get the ball in the **service box** diagonally across the net from her. The server begins each game by serving from the right side of the court. Servers must stand behind the baseline and between the **center mark** and the singles sideline.

Molly has two chances to get a serve in. If both attempts land outside the box or in the net (a **double fault**), Molly loses the point. Molly must stay behind the baseline until she hits the ball. If she crosses the line before the ball is hit (**foot fault**), the serve is called out even if it lands in the correct service box. Molly has served an **ace** if her opponent can't return the serve.

Before each serve, the server must call out the score loud enough so that the opponent can hear it. This way, players keep track of the score.

After the point is played, Molly switches to the other side of the center mark and serves to the other service box. The server switches sides after each point.

The Returner

The returner can stand anywhere on his or her side of the court. Heidi watches the lines carefully from behind the baseline. If Molly misses the serve, Heidi must yell out loudly, "Fault." If the serve lands in, Heidi must try to hit the ball across the net to Molly's singles court.

Umpires

Tennis umpires can take three roles in any tournament. Some umpires are roving umpires. These umpires roam about a tournament site, keeping an eye on many courts at one time. They help players with any problems that they have during play.

Other umpires are called line umpires. You have seen these umpires in tennis matches on TV. Line umpires sit along the various lines on a tennis court and call the balls in or out on that line. Line umpires can only call balls that land on or near their own particular line.

A chair umpire sits at the net in a chair and is responsible for the whole tennis court. The chair umpire keeps score and helps the players through any problems that arise during a match. The chair umpire also corrects any line calls that are incorrect during a match.

When any umpire is on or near your court, you should treat him or her with respect. Umpires do a great service for the game of tennis. Many times on TV you will see a professional player yelling at an umpire. This should never happen in a tennis match and usually only shows a player's inability to handle the pressures of a match. Treat all umpires with respect.

Singles Strategy

There are many strategies in a game of tennis. All players play tennis in a unique way. Here are a few tips on how to become a better player faster.

Even at the professional level, most points are scored because of errors, not great shots. A common error is hitting the ball too hard. Your goal should be to get one more ball in play than your opponent does each time. If you can do that, you will be the next All-American doing tennis shoe commercials on TV.

Many mistakes end up in the net. It's better to miss your shots either deep or wide. Missing the shot deep behind the baseline at least means you are using the correct stroke (low-to-high) and hitting the ball solidly on the strings.

When you feel you can control the ball, find out your opponent's weaknesses. Does he or she make more errors on the forehand or backhand side? If you find a weakness, try to hit all of your balls toward that weaker side.

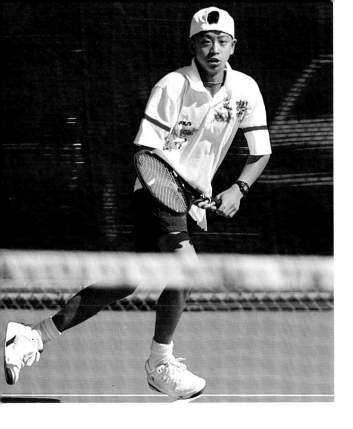

Finally, think about defense. Many times you will be scrambling around, trying to get to your opponent's shots. Remember, good players do not make many mistakes, so when you are hitting defensive balls, hit softly and well inside all of the lines to keep the ball in play.

At the end of every match, go to the net and shake your opponent's hand. Whether you win or lose, find something good to say about how your opponent played. Sometimes this is hard to do, especially if you lose a close match. Keep in mind that you cannot become a better player unless you play against better players. Learn something from every match that you play, win or lose.

Finally, thank your mom or dad or brother or sister for bringing you to play this match and for watching you play. If it was a practice, tell them thanks for giving you the chance to improve. Those who help you need to hear "Thanks" every day!

Chapter 4

DOUBLES

Doubles is a team game, with two players playing together, moving together, thinking together, and winning together. The most important ingredient in any successful doubles team is the players' ability to communicate with each other.

The rules for doubles play are the same as those for singles. The scoring is also the same. However, the size of the court is different. When playing doubles, the players can use the doubles alleys also. This means that the court is 36 feet wide instead of 27 feet wide. Although the court is wider, the service box stays the same size.

The Serving Team

The serving team begins the match with either player serving first. This person serves for the entire game. Once a game is finished, the other team serves. Teammates alternate serving games for the rest of the set. Either player may begin serving at the beginning of a new set. The server usually stands between the center mark and the doubles line. The server's partner stands in the middle of the service box that is not in front of the server.

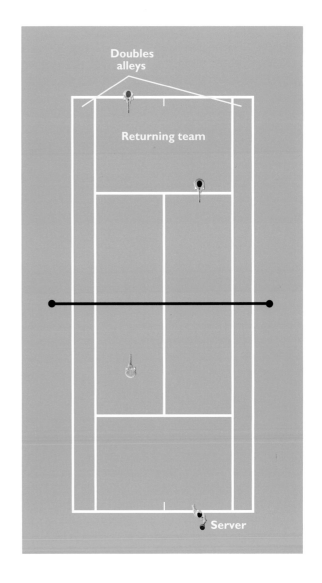

43

The Returning Team

The returning team can choose which player will return from the forehand side and which player will return from the backhand side. Players position themselves so they will hit their best shots from the middle of the court, because most balls are hit down the middle in a doubles match. Once a set begins, the players must start on their side for the remainder of that set. At the completion of the set, the players may change sides.

Phil and Mary are preparing to return serve. Phil is at the baseline and Mary is at the service line. When players begin a match in this way, they are in the one-up and one-back position.

In this position, the two players have clear roles. The forward, or up, person is the attacker and will try to move across the net and hit as many volleys as possible. The back person is like a center fielder. This player is responsible for covering behind the net person and hitting a lot of balls back.

Doubles Strategy

The back person must understand that it is almost impossible to hit winning points from the baseline. Most points will be won from a position close to the net. Because of this, the back person should run to the net as soon in the point as he or she can. The strongest position that a doubles team can be in is with both players at the net.

Because the net player can volley so effectively, hit balls to the back person whenever possible. When Charlie hits the ball down the alley to Phil, Phil will easily put the ball away between Charlie and Molly. Look at the size of the hole between Charlie and Molly. There is no way that they can cover all of this space, so Phil can score. If both players are at the net, there is much less space between them.

If a team comes to the net against you, hit the ball over their heads with a **lob** (high shot) or drive balls down the middle between them.

The lob, which we'll talk about more in the last chapter, is a shot that is hit high over the net players. When you hit a lob over your opponents, both you and your partner should run toward the net, but do not run too close in or your opponents will lob the ball over you!

The lob is one of the most effective shots in doubles because it keeps the ball away from the net person, who will put most of the balls away. Charlie is lobbing over Mary's head and following the lob to the net. Phil is turning to chase the lob and his partner, Mary, is switching sides. This is how teammates cover the lob.

Charlie lobs over Mary's head.

Phil runs back after the lob...

...as Mary moves to cover his side of the court.

Phil prepares to return the lob.

Another strategy to use against a team at the net is driving balls down the middle between the two players, because that's their weakest spot. Charlie is hitting the ball between Phil and Mary and neither can cover the shot. Even if they were able to cover Charlie's shot, they do not have a good angle to put away the ball.

It is very important that the two players communicate with each other. The players should talk to each other during points. If you feel that you can hit the ball, call loudly, "Mine." This tells your partner that you'll get the ball,

and he or she is free to move into position to cover your opponent's return.

Teammates also should talk between points. Try to get together as a team. Know what your partner is thinking. Try to figure out what your opponents are thinking. Discover your opponents' weaknesses. Which one is the stronger player? Try to hit most of the balls to the other player.

Find a partner you enjoy and play some doubles. You'll have someone with whom to share your triumphs and disappointments. Doubles is a game that everyone should try!

Chapter 5

PRACTICE, PRACTICE

Once you have learned a little bit about tennis, you will want to practice so that you can improve your skills. What do you do? How do you get the most out of the time you spend working on your tennis game?

First, decide which skill or skills need work. If you try to make all of your skills great at the same time, none of them will develop very much. If you take one or two strokes and become comfortable with them, and then work on the other strokes, you will develop a solid game.

Practice Progression

Mary and Heidi are doing some drills that all young players can do. Mary stands next to Heidi and drops the ball at Heidi's side. Heidi hits the balls at a target on the other side of the net. Heidi hits 10 or 15 balls over the net, and then Heidi drops balls for Mary. In this drill, Heidi is having great success and continues to practice. Also, Heidi is able to think about her stroke because the action is slower than in a match and fairly easy to do. If Heidi were scrambling for every ball while trying to hit, she would have very little time to think about her strokes.

Practice Success

Your practice time can be a blast! Chasing balls around and smacking them over the net is fun. So is sweating a little while you and your partner improve your skills.

So why do some young players avoid practicing? Because standing at the baseline and hitting balls back and forth with your partner is difficult when you are a beginner. After one or two hits you will have to go pick up the balls.

Instead, try building on each skill you master. Don't try to do another skill until you can successfully perform the one on which you are working. Take your time and learn the basic skills well. Build a strong base with your strokes. You will have the most fun when you are hitting the balls over the net and into the court. Keep it simple!

Tossing to Each Other

After both girls have hit many balls over the net, Mary backs up about 10 feet. Now she is off to the side so that she will not get hit by Heidi's forehand shots. Mary tosses these balls so Heidi can stroke them easily over the net. Heidi again hits 10 or 15 over the net to a target and then switches positions with Mary. To make this tougher, Mary tosses the balls so that Heidi has to run a few steps before she hits the ball.

Feeding Each Other

Once each player can do that drill, the players can hit by themselves. Heidi takes a ball, drops it, and hits it to Mary. Mary catches the ball and tosses it back to Heidi. When Heidi can drop a ball and hit it to Mary well enough that Mary can practice her stroke, Heidi is feeding Mary.

As the players get better at this drill, they can practice feeding each other. This helps the players get used to seeing tennis balls come off the racket. As a player's skill level increases, he or she is able to react more quickly to the ball that the opponent is hitting.

Rallying

Once Heidi and Mary can successfully feed each other, they are ready to **rally**. Rallying is when two players hit the ball back and forth over the net without the ball stopping. When Heidi and Mary begin to rally, they start at the service line instead of at the baseline. This keeps the pace of the balls a little slower and allows them to have longer rallies with more hits. When they can hit 10 or 15 balls over the net without a miss, they move back to the baseline and rally using the whole court.

Practicing with a Wall

Many times a player will want to practice, but no court or partner is available. Then, the perfect practice partner is a wall or backboard. When you practice against the wall, keep the same idea in mind: "Be successful!" Drop the ball and hit to a target, then catch the ball as it bounces off the wall.

When you can do this five times in a row without a miss, drop the ball and hit the wall again. But as the ball bounces back to you, hit it back to the wall toward your target. To hit the ball back, you will have to get ready immediately after each hit. If you stand and watch your ball going to the wall, it will bounce on the wall and sail back to you before you can react. Try to keep the ball going for 5 to 10 hits in a row. Do not worry about hitting the ball very hard. Keeping the ball going and hitting the strokes with good form is more important. Be patient, keep your practicing simple, and stay with it.

Fitness

How important is fitness to a tennis player? Very important! Fitness involves several different areas for a tennis player. Strength, endurance, speed, quickness, balance, and flexibility are all equally important. Tennis requires a player to be able to hit while moving, stop and change positions quickly, cover the court rapidly, and hit the ball hard with accuracy.

Warm-up

Warm up each time that you go out to play or practice tennis. Warming up can be done with jogging, jumping rope, or any other activity that will work up a little sweat. Once you have warmed up, you can begin stretching.

Conditioning

Players should know what they want to improve before beginning any conditioning exercises. There are two types of conditioning that can be done by a player through exercise drills, **aerobic** and **anaerobic conditioning**.

Aerobic conditioning—long-distance exercising—builds up a player's endurance and stamina. Examples of aerobic conditioning are jogging, bicycling, and swimming. Aerobic conditioning is usually done for at least 20 minutes.

Anaerobic conditioning builds a player's explosiveness and power. Examples of anaerobic conditioning are sprinting, hopping, jumping, and quick line drills with frequent changes of direction. Anaerobic conditioning is usually done for 30 seconds to one minute, with 30 seconds of rest between drills.

Strength Training

Strength can be improved by resistance training. Resistance training refers to exercises in which some resistance is added to movement to overload specific muscles. When a muscle is overloaded, it rebuilds itself and becomes stronger than it was before. All resistance training should be supervised by a knowledgeable professional or coach. Resistance training includes many different types of exercises that require many different machines and equipment.

Chapter 6

Bjorn Borg

Bjorn Borg was born in Sodertalje, Sweden, and grew up aspiring to be a hockey player. Bjorn's father was one of the best table tennis players in Sweden, and Bjorn played table tennis too. When Bjorn was 9 years old, his father gave him a tennis racket. Bjorn began to play tennis. He hit balls with topspin, the way table tennis players do. Topspin makes the ball rotate forward in the direction it is going. Balls hit with topspin tend to drop sharply. Bjorn hit forehands with a Western grip. He hit his backhands with a two-handed grip. By doing this, he was able to generate a lot of topspin on all of his shots.

When Bjorn was 15 years old, he was selected to play on the Swedish Davis Cup team. Bjorn won the French Open when he was 17. When he turned 19, he won the first of his five Wimbledon Championships. Bjorn Borg, "the Ice Man," is still remembered for his fierce topspin and his icy cool behavior on the court.

RAZZLE DAZZLE

As your skills become more advanced, you can learn to play at the net. From the net, you can finish points by hitting balls to places where your opponents are not. If you stay at the baseline all of the time, you must rely on the other player making the mistakes. Hitting outright winners from the baseline is very difficult.

The Lob

Because better players come to the net more often, they must add a few skills to their games. The first skill is the **lob**. There are two reasons to hit a lob. First, hit a lob against a player who is coming to the net. The goal is to hit the ball over your opponent's head when he or she is at the net and make him or her retreat to the baseline, giving you a chance to get to the net.

55

Second, you often will be pulled out of position by an opponent's shot. In order to create more time to recover your court position, you can lob the ball high into the air. While the ball floats up and comes down, you will have time to recover your position. For these reasons, the lob is a necessary technique.

Molly is hitting a lob. In her preparation, her racket is well below the ball. As Molly swings at the ball, her racket face is open. The lob is different from a ground stroke because when hitting the lob, Molly will make contact with the ball on the bottom side of the ball. This makes the ball sail high into the air.

Molly finishes this stroke with her arm high above her head as her racket extends to her target.

The target for the lob is important. A lob is a shot that follows the shape of a rainbow. The highest point in a lob's "rainbow" is directly over the net. The ball will sail up, come to its peak above the net, and then land near the opponent's baseline. If the peak of the rainbow is over Molly's side, the lob will be short and her opponent will have an easy shot. If the peak of the rainbow is over her opponent's side of the court, the ball will land beyond the baseline and will be out. The peak of the rainbow must be near the center of the court over the net.

The Overhead

The **overhead** shot is hit when you are at the net. Phil has come to the net. His opponent is trying to drive Phil to the baseline by hitting a lob over his head. Instead of running to the baseline and letting the ball bounce, Phil is going to hit the ball while it is in the air above his head. This is called an overhead.

Positioning on the overhead is important. Phil's racket hand is behind his head in the back-scratch position and his other hand is up in the air, searching for the ball. If Phil were to let the ball fall and not hit it, he would be able to catch the ball in this hand. This is the exact position Phil should be in to hit the overhead.

The point of contact for the overhead is nearly the same as for the serve. The ball should be hit as high as Phil can reach with his racket and a little bit in front of his body. Notice that Phil's eyes are focused on the ball at the point of contact. Phil will finish the overhead with his racket hand across his body.

The drop shot is different from the ground strokes. It is almost a baby lob, which you hit very short and which lands just over the net. Mary is preparing for this shot. Her eyes are on the ball and her racket face is slightly open, as for a lob. Her swing is very short because she wants to hit the ball short—in fact, just over the net. But notice how her finish ends up high again. Most people trying to hit the ball short wind up hitting the ball into the net. This is because they end the shot with a short, low finish. Hitting a drop shot from near the baseline is difficult because the ball needs to travel too far in the air before it crosses the net. The best place from which to hit the drop shot is near the service line, where a soft little shot can just sneak over the net. Keep in mind that you are not trying to win the point on the drop shot. All you are trying to do is bring your opponent to the net with a fairly difficult ball. Once he or she is at the net, you can lob or force volleys. Either way, you are making your opponent do something other than hit ground strokes, which is what he or she wants to do.

The Drop Shot

Another shot related to net play is the **drop shot**. The drop shot is used to force an opponent to run toward the net for short balls. Let's say that you are playing against an opponent who has great forehands and backhands. Your opponent is beating you on too many points from the baseline. But you noticed in the warm-up session that your opponent's volleys were not very solid. You would like to get your opponent to the net and force him or her to hit volleys. The drop shot is the shot that you hit.

Being a Winner

Tennis is fun whether you're smashing overheads at Wimbledon or running your brother ragged with drop shots. Millions of people stay fit and have fun on the tennis court. Now you can be one of them.

TENNIS TALK

ace: A serve that an opponent doesn't return.

ad-in: The score when the server wins a point to break a 40-40 tie in a game.

ad-out: The score when the server's opponent wins a point to break a 40-40 score in a game.

aerobic conditioning: Developing endurance with exercises that increase your heart rate and breathing rate, such as jogging and swimming.

anaerobic conditioning: Developing strength with exercises that increase your muscle strength, such as weight lifting.

back-scratch position: The point during a serve when the racket head is at the middle of your back.

backhand: A ground stroke hit by reaching across your body so that the back of your hand swings out at the ball; can be done with one or two hands.

baseline: The line parallel to the net that marks the end of the court.

center mark: A short mark in the center of the baseline that defines the service area.

court: Flat rectangular area on which tennis is played; 78 feet long; 27 feet wide for playing singles, 36 feet wide for doubles; divided by a 3-foot high net.

crosscourt: From one corner of the court to the corner diagonally across.

deuce: Tie score of 40 points each.

double fault: Both serving attempts by a player land outside the service box or in the net.

doubles alleys: Areas 4½ feet wide on each side of the court used when playing doubles.

doubles sidelines: Lines on the court marking the doubles alleys.

doubles: Tennis played by four players, two against two.

drop shot: A short shot that lands just over the net.

fast courts: Courts with surfaces, such as grass, that are slick.

finish: A player's position after a stroke has been completed.

foot fault: A server steps on or over the baseline before the ball is hit.

forehand: A ground stroke hit on the same side of the body as the hand holding the racket, so that the palm of the hand swings toward the ball.

game: A series of four or more points, with one player scoring at least two more points than an opponent.

grip: The way a player holds a racket in his or her hand.

ground stroke: Any stroke used after the ball has bounced on your side of the court.

let: A ball that hits the top of the net and lands on the other side of the court; also the term used to call for a replay if another ball or object is on the court during play.

lob: A high, arching shot.

love: Scoring term for zero.

match: Three sets; the first player to win two sets wins the match. (Male professional tennis players play best-of-five-set matches.)

mis-hit: When the ball is hit with the frame of the racket instead of with the face.

overhead: Hard swing from above your head at an opponent's shot, much as for a serve, but hit during a point.

point of contact: Where the ball and the racket meet.

racket: A lightweight bat with a long handle and netting stretched across an open oval frame.

rally: Players hitting the ball back and forth over the net without the ball stopping.

ready position: The stance your body is in while waiting to hit a shot; knees bent, weight slightly on the balls of your feet, your racket loose and about waist high.

recover: To regain your balance and position after you hit a shot.

serve: The stroke used to put the ball in play at the start of each point in a game.

service box: The rectangle marked off on the court by the net, the service lines, and the sideline, that is diagonally across the net from the server.

service line: The line 21 feet from the net that defines the service box.

set: Six or more games, with one player winning at least two games more than his or her opponent.

singles sidelines: The lines that define the sides of the court for singles play.

singles: Tennis played by two players, one against one.

slow courts: Courts with rough surfaces, like clay, which slow down the ball and give it a higher bounce.

stance: A player's beginning position for a stroke.

stroke: Movement of the racket designed to hit the ball over the net and in the court on the other side.

tie-breaker: A 12-point play-off to decide the winner of a set after both players have won six games. One player must win at least seven points and at least two more than his or her opponent.

V position: The point during a serve when your racket is raised above your head and your other arm has just released the ball for the toss.

volley: Any shot that is used to hit the ball before it bounces.

FURTHER READING

Braden, Vic and Bill Bruns. *Vic Braden's Quick Fixes*. Boston, Massachusetts: Little Brown, 1988.

Gallwey, W. Timothy. *The Inner Game of Tennis*. New York: Random House, Inc., 1974.

Klotz, Donald D. *Tennis — Keep it Simple*. Dubuque, Iowa: William C. Brown Publishers, 1989.

Lappin, Greg. *Tennis Doubles*. Edina, Minnesota: KC Books Company, 1985.

Lee, Simon. *Play the Game Tennis*. Great Britain: Ward Lock Limited, 1988.

Lloyd, David. *Fit for the Game Tennis*. Great Britain: Ward Lock Limited, 1991.

Loehr, James E. *The Mental Game*. New York: S. Greene Press, 1990.

Scott, Eugen L. *Bjorn Borg, My Life and My Game*. New York: Simon & Schuster, 1980.

Smith, Jay H. *Chris Evert*. Mankato, Minnesota: Creative Educational Society, Inc., 1975.

FOR MORE INFORMATION

Association of Tennis Professionals (ATP)
611 Ryan Plaza Drive
Suite 620
Arlington, TX 76011

International Tennis Federation (ITF)
Church Road
Wimbledon, London, England SW19 5TF

The National Collegiate Athletic Association (NCAA)
6201 College Boulevard
Overland Park, KS 66211-2422

United States Professional Tennis Association (USPTA)
One USPTA Centre
3535 Briarpark Drive
Houston, TX 77042

United States Professional Tennis Registry (USPTR)
PO Box 4739
Hilton Head, SC 29938

United States Tennis Association (USTA)
70 West Red Oak Lane
White Plains, NY 10604-3602

INDEX